NATIONAL
GEOGRAPHIC

T0045238

# Hands at Work

Freya Purdey

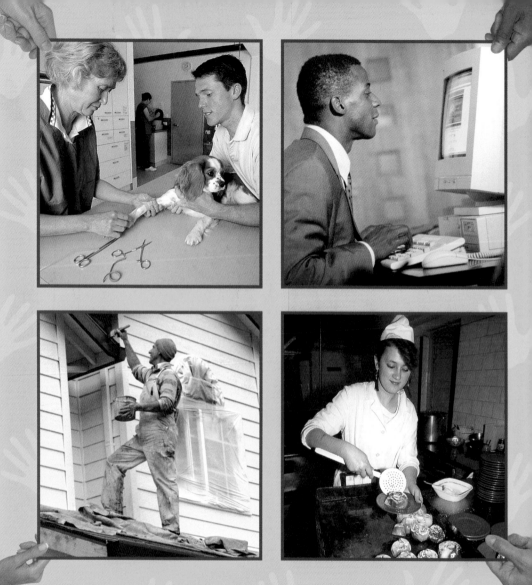

People use their hands at work.

2

Who is at work?

3

The doctor is at work.

Who is at work?

5

The gardener is at work.

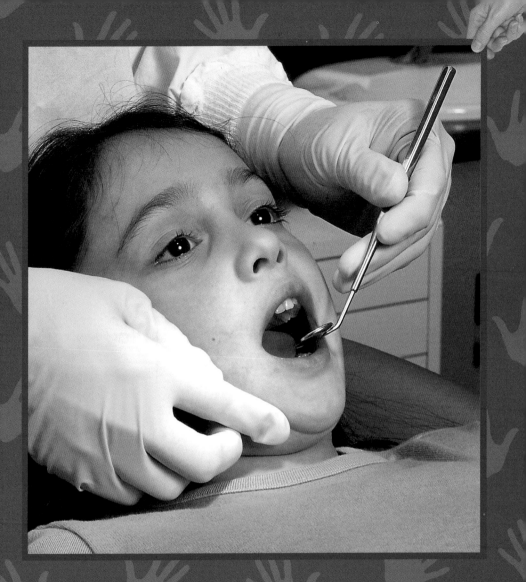

Who is at work?

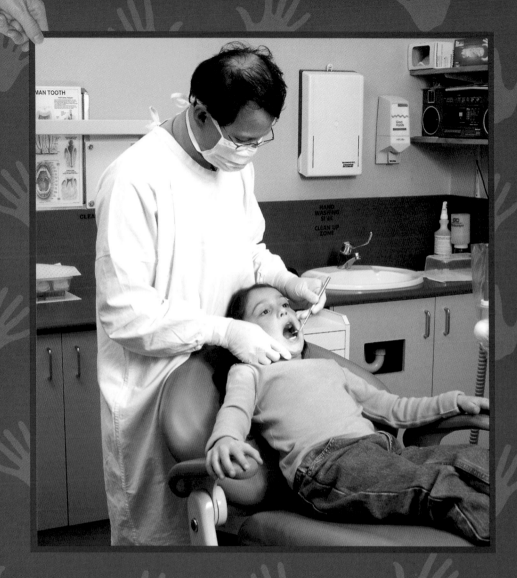

The dentist is at work.

8

Who is at work?

9

The carpenter is at work.

10

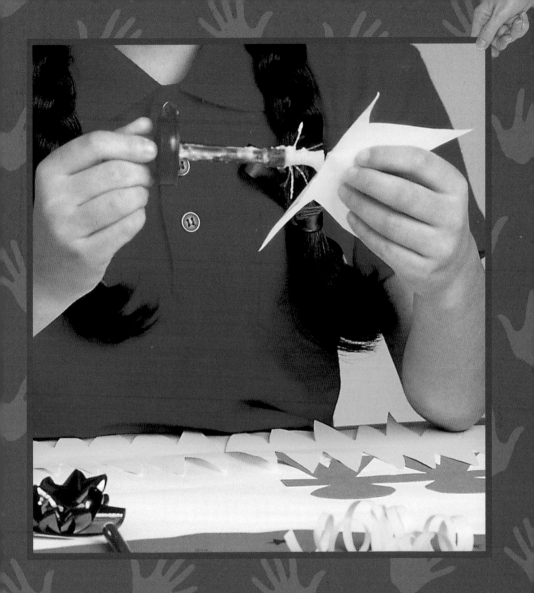

Who is at work?

I am at work.

12